A Map of My House

by Katherine Scraper

I need to know these words.

hall

kitchen

living room

map

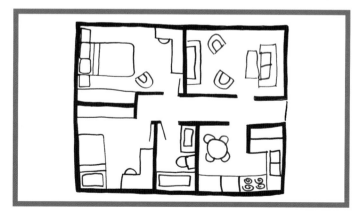

I have a map of
my house.

5

The kitchen is in my house.

The kitchen is on my map.

The hall is in my house.

The hall is on my map.

The bathroom is in my house.

The bathroom is on my map.

The bedroom is in my house.

The bedroom is on
my map.

The living room is on my map.

The living room is in my house.

My family is in my house.